FARMING ENCYCLOPEDIAS

THE CROP ENCYCLOPEDIA

BY ANGELA LIM

Encyclopedias

An Imprint of Abdo Reference

abdobooks.com

TABLE OF CONTENTS

HISTORY OF US AGRICULTURE

Agriculture has been an important industry in the United States (US) since before the founding of the country. Until the 1850s, farmers used hand tools such as hoes and sickles to tend to their crops. But over time, new technologies developed. Tools such as mechanical plows and reapers made it quicker and easier to plant and harvest crops.

The US government has long worked to improve agriculture and help farmers. President Abraham Lincoln created the US Department of Agriculture (USDA) in 1862. At that time, approximately 90 percent of Americans were farmers. Today, the USDA supports farmers by providing guidelines on how to manage land and improve nutrition in foods.

The agricultural industry continued changing in the 1900s. New farming machines made it possible to farm large areas of land. Large farms began to replace small, independent ones. The Great Depression, a period of economic downturn that started in 1929 and lasted for a decade, also caused many small farms to shut down.

US AGRICULTURE TODAY

In 2021, the United States had about 2 million farms. The average size of a US farm was 445 acres (180 ha). Agriculture is a major industry that is worth more than $1 trillion in the United States.

In addition to better farming machines, other developments have boosted the industry. Pesticides prevent crops from being eaten by insects. Herbicides limit the growth of weeds, which can take nutrients away from crops. These chemicals allow farms to be more productive and have larger harvests. But they can also harm wildlife and damage the environment.

Fertilizers have also improved crop yields. These products add nutrients to the soil and help crops grow quickly. However, fertilizers can wash into waterways. They can harm wildlife and make water sources dangerous to drink.

The US agricultural industry grows many different types of crops. Food crops provide nutrition to people around the world. Feed crops are fed to animals such as cows, pigs, and chickens. People process fiber crops to make textiles and fabrics. Oil crops are used to make oils for cooking and fuel. Farming is a major part of US history, and it remains a key sector of the country's economy today.

Millions of farmers across the United States grow crops that provide food, fuel, textiles, and many other products.

FOOD CROPS

California has about 1.6 million acres (648,000 ha) of almond orchards.

ALMONDS

Almonds are nuts that grow on trees. The trees typically blossom in February or March. Honeybees pollinate the flowers, which then develop into almonds. The nuts have a tough outer shell. People eat the softer insides of the nuts.

Almond trees grow in loamy, clay-like soil. They need a lot of sunlight and water. These trees do best in temperatures from 59 to 86 degrees Fahrenheit (15 to 30°C).

The blossoms of the almond tree are sometimes used for decorative purposes.

GROWING ALMONDS

The United States is the largest producer of almonds. It grows 78 percent of the world's total crop. In 2022 the worldwide demand for almonds was projected to continue growing through the late 2020s. In the United States, the almond industry is worth approximately $5.5 billion. California is the only US state where almonds are grown commercially.

Almonds are popular nuts with a wide variety of uses.

HARVEST

Almond trees are harvested during the fall. Farmers use special machinery to harvest the nuts. A shaking machine has a claw that grasps the trunk of an almond tree and shakes it. The movement causes the almonds to fall. The claw has a protective cover so that it does not damage the tree.

The fallen almonds are left on the ground to dry for four to seven days. Then a sweeping machine piles the nuts into rows. This makes it easier for a harvesting machine to gather them. Then the harvesting machine vacuums up the almonds. As it does this, it separates the nuts from soil and other unwanted materials.

More almonds are harvested than can be processed in facilities. The extra almonds are stored in stockpiles. The nuts

Almonds fly through the air as the shaking machine vibrates the tree trunk.

are treated with chemicals to remove harmful germs. The stockpiles are then sealed under tarps, where they are stored until they can be processed.

USES

Almonds are used in a variety of food products. They can be added to baked goods and desserts. They may be included in breakfast foods such as cereals or granola bars.

Sometimes processing is minimal. Almonds can be sold in-shell. They may also be processed to remove shells. Other processing steps include chopping and roasting. Almonds can also be combined with sugar and made into a paste called marzipan. This sweet paste is commonly used in desserts and candies.

Almonds can also be made into flour. Most flour is made from wheat, which contains a protein called gluten. People with a condition called celiac disease are sensitive to gluten. Almond flour and other nut flours do not have gluten, which makes them good alternatives for those with celiac disease. To make almond flour, almonds are shelled and boiled. The boiled almonds are then ground and sifted.

Almonds with a honey coating can make a sweet, protein-rich snack bar.

Almond milk is available in sweetened and unsweetened varieties.

Almond milk is another almond product. It is an alternative for people who do not drink dairy milk. Some people cannot drink animal milk because of medical conditions. Other people follow a vegan diet and do not consume animal products. Almond milk is easy to make. It can even be made at home. Almonds are blended with water. The mixture is then strained to remove solids.

Apple producers in Washington State harvest between 10 and 12 billion apples each year.

APPLES

Apples are fruits that grow on trees. For an apple tree to produce fruit, its flowers, known as blossoms, need to receive pollen from another apple tree. Flying insects such as bees carry pollen between trees. Apple orchards typically have crab apple trees that provide pollen for other apple tree varieties. Crab apple flowers attract many pollinators. Growing times vary depending on the variety, but apple trees typically bloom in the spring and produce fruit in late summer or fall.

Growing conditions influence fruit quality. Apple trees require eight hours of sun a day. These trees should be spaced apart when they are planted. If trees are crowded together, they will grow in each other's shade. Taller trees need more

space than shorter ones. Apple trees also need a lot of water, especially when they are young. They grow best in loamy soil.

It takes a lot of nutrients to grow fruit. Farmers often pick some apples before a tree is ready for harvest. By removing some apples, the tree can give more nutrients to the remaining fruit. The apples will be able to grow larger.

Young apple trees are managed carefully to promote healthy growth.

More than 2,500 types of apples are grown in the United States. Some of the major apple varieties include Red Delicious, Gala, Granny Smith, and Fuji. In 2021, approximately 10.5 billion pounds (4.8 billion kg) of apples were harvested in the United States. Washington State is the nation's top producer of apples.

APPLE VARIETIES

When an apple blossom is pollinated, it receives genes from the tree that produced the pollen. The genes of the two trees combine. Genes are the instructions that living things use to grow and develop. Genes also influence characteristics of the apple, such as its juiciness and sweetness.

Apple varieties can be significantly different from each other in color, taste, and texture.

Popular apple varieties are grown in huge numbers.

Apple breeders think about the traits they want their apples to have. They can plant apple trees with these traits close to each other. For example, the creators of the Cosmic Crisp apple wanted an apple that was firm, crisp, and juicy. Enterprise apples are firm and crisp. Honeycrisp apples are known for their juiciness. These trees were bred together. Seeds from the most promising fruit were collected and planted. After more than 20 years of breeding, farmers produced the Cosmic Crisp.

Once an apple variety has been established, orchard farmers no longer use seeds to grow new trees. Instead, they use a method called clonal propagation. This technique involves cutting a branch with buds from the apple tree. When planted, this branch continues to grow and bear fruit.

Harvesting apples is done by hand, but machines can make the work of gathering them easier.

Apple pie is one of the many popular food products made with apples.

HARVEST AND PROCESSING

Apples bruise easily, so people must pick them by hand. The fruits are loaded into bins and taken to sorting and packaging facilities. Machines scan the apples and remove bruised and damaged ones. The fruits are kept at temperatures just above freezing as they are packaged and shipped. This prevents the apples from spoiling.

Apples are the most-consumed fruit in the United States. Most apples are eaten fresh, without additional processing. About one-third of apples are grown to be used in products such as apple juice, apple cider, and applesauce.

CITRUS

Citrus crops grown in the United States include oranges, grapefruit, limes, and lemons. These fruits grow on trees. Citrus trees typically do not survive if temperatures fall below 28 degrees Fahrenheit (–2°C) for an extended amount of time. They also need more than six hours of sunlight a day throughout the year.

In 2022, Florida and California combined grew more than 450,000 acres (182,000 ha) of oranges.

Grapefruit are known for their tart and tangy taste.

Citrus trees need to be watered once or twice a week. Young trees should be watered more often. Citrus trees grow best in soil that drains water well. The soil should be moist but not soaked.

Because citrus trees require warm temperatures, they are grown only in the southern United States. California and Florida are the primary growers of citrus fruits. Together, these two states produced 96 percent of US citrus in 2020.

CITRUS DECLINES

The US citrus industry faced declines in the early 2020s. This drop was largely due to recent struggles with growing citrus in Florida. In 2022, the state reported its lowest citrus production since the 1940s. Climate change caused an increase in hurricanes and tropical storms, weather events that affect citrus growth.

Asian citrus psyllids present a major challenge to citrus growers.

Florida citrus has also been impacted by the Asian citrus psyllids. These insects are native to Asia. They feed on citrus plants. The insects inject toxins into the plants as they feed, causing leaves to blacken and die. They have been in Florida since 1998.

Asian citrus psyllids also carry a disease called huanglongbing (HLB). This disease can affect all types of citrus, and there is no cure. It first causes yellow spots to appear on citrus leaves. As the disease worsens, fruit becomes smaller and remains

The effects of HLB can be seen in fruit that remains green after it is supposed to ripen.

partially green. For this reason, HLB is sometimes called citrus greening. Eventually HLB causes the tree to die. HLB was first detected in Florida in 2005 and has since spread to other US states. Pesticides that kill the Asian citrus psyllid help stop the spread of HLB.

HARVEST

Most citrus fruits ripen during the winter. However, some varieties of orange are harvested during the summer. Lemons and limes are harvested year-round.

Farmers may use machinery to harvest citrus crops, including grapefruit.

Large orchards use machines to harvest citrus. The use of canopy shakers in the United States began increasing in the early 2000s. These machines grasp the trunk of the tree. A catch frame expands around the tree. The machine shakes the tree, causing fruit to fall onto the catch frame. The frame funnels the citrus crops to a collection compartment.

USES

Citrus fruits can be eaten without processing. But they can also be processed to make products such as juice. In 2021, 57 percent of US citrus was processed. Orange juice is one of the country's main citrus exports.

Machinery presses or crushes the fruit to collect juice. The juice may be pulpy after this step. It is filtered to remove solids.

Next, sugars may be added. The juice is also treated so that it stays fresh for as long as possible. This step involves removing gases from the liquid and heating the juice to kill germs.

Orange juice is high in vitamin C but also contains a lot of sugar.

CORN

Corn is planted in rows during the spring. It needs a lot of space to grow. Corn grows best in full sun and nutrient-rich soil. Cornstalks have shallow roots, so the plants suffer quickly in droughts. They need a significant amount of water to survive.

Corn is native to the Americas. Thousands of years ago, it started as a wild grass called teosinte. Ears of teosinte were

Planting corn in straight rows maximizes the amount of the crop that farmers can get out of their land.

Modern ears of corn are dramatically larger than their teosinte ancestors.

very small and had few kernels. American Indian farmers selectively bred teosinte. They planted kernels from plants that had the largest ears. Over time, this created the corn that is grown today.

Many types of corn are grown in the United States. Sweet corn is the main type of corn that people eat. But only about 10 percent of US corn is used in foods for people. Most corn is fed to animals or used to produce fuel.

Scientists have changed the genes of some types of corn. These corn varieties are genetically modified organisms (GMOs). Modifying a crop's genes results in changes to its growth and development. Most types of GMO corn are created to be resistant to pests,

The Midwest has ideal conditions for growing corn.

such as insects. Genetic modifications can cause the corn to produce a protein that is toxic to some insects. But this protein does not affect humans, pets, or livestock.

GROWING CORN

Every US state grows corn. The majority is grown in the Midwest. Iowa and Illinois are the top producers of corn. Together, they account for about one-third of the country's corn harvest.

HARVEST

Farmers harvest corn in the fall. Each stalk of sweet corn has one or two ears. Corn is considered both a vegetable and a grain. Early in the harvesting season, its nutritional value is similar to a vegetable. Corn becomes starchier and grain-like toward the end of fall.

Farmers commonly use machines such as combines and silage harvesters to harvest corn. These machines have

Heavy machinery helps farmers quickly and efficiently harvest huge amounts of corn.

specialized parts that help them efficiently harvest a specific crop. Machines used to harvest corn are designed to collect corn from multiple rows at a time. They have blades that chop the cornstalk. The cut stalks fall to the ground, and the machines collect the corncobs.

FOOD USES

Sweet corn can be eaten straight off the cob. Other types of corn require more processing before they can be consumed.

A substance called high-fructose corn syrup is widely used to sweeten beverages such as soda.

Field corn, or dent corn, is used to make cornstarch. Cornstarch is commonly used to thicken gravies and sauces. When cornstarch is heated with acid or mixed with proteins called enzymes, it produces corn syrup. Corn syrup accounts for about one-third of corn food products. It is sweet and used in products such as candies and jams. Other corn products include tortillas and corn chips. These are often made from white corn.

Popcorn is a separate variety of corn. Popcorn strains have different flavors. The kernels are dried for eight to twelve months. Pressure builds up inside the kernels when they are heated. The pressure causes the kernels to pop, creating the popular snack.

Americans eat about 17 billion quarts (18.7 million cubic m) of popcorn each year.

CRANBERRIES

Cranberries grow low to the ground.

Cranberries are fruits that are native to North America. They grow on sprawling shrubs. These plants require full sun but cool temperatures. They grow best in acidic soil. Adding peat moss to the soil helps keep it acidic. Cranberries need a lot of water and can survive floods.

Wisconsin is the top producer of cranberries in the United States. In 2021, it accounted for 59 percent of the country's crop. Cranberries are a billion-dollar industry in the state.

HARVEST

Cranberries turn a deep red color when they are ready to harvest. Farmers use two methods to harvest cranberries—dry and wet harvesting. During a dry harvest, farmers use raking machines. These are pushed like lawn mowers. As the machine travels over the shrubs, it chops cranberries from the plants.

The cranberries are collected in a sack at the back of the machine.

Wet harvesting accounts for about 90 percent of US cranberry harvests. Before the harvest begins, farmers flood the area where the cranberries are growing with 18 to 24 inches (46 to 61 cm) of water.

Farmers usually flood a cranberry field, forming a bog where the fruits will be harvested.

Twelve hours later, the harvesting begins. First, farmers use long rods called water reels to stir the water and shake the cranberries loose. The cranberries float on the water's surface. Farmers gather the fruit. They use pumps to load the cranberries onto trucks, and the berries are taken away for further processing.

Specialized machinery helps workers efficiently harvest the cranberries.

More than 70 million cans of cranberry sauce are sold each year in the United States.

USES

Cranberries from dry harvests are sold fresh. Cranberries from wet harvests are used to make many food products. Some examples include juices, sauces, and jellies.

Cranberry sauce is popular for Thanksgiving meals. It can be bought in stores, but it can also be made at home. The cranberries are mixed with water and sugar is added. Then the mixture is brought to a boil. Cranberries contain a chemical called pectin that gives the mixture a jelly-like texture once it cools.

The practice of growing grapes is known as viticulture.

GRAPES

Grapes are fruits that grow on vines. Left unpruned, grapevines can grow up to 115 feet (35 m) long. However, the quality of the fruit suffers when vines get too long.

Grapevines need about eight hours of sunlight every day. Low amounts of sunlight can lead to smaller harvests. These plants grow in a variety of soils but have deep roots. They should not be planted in areas where large rocks are less than 4 feet (1.2 m) underground. Young grapes need

about 1 inch (2.5 cm) of water each week. After two years, grapes do not need to be watered as frequently.

More than 80 types of grapes are grown in the United States. California produces more than 99 percent of US grapes. The state's grapes are shipped worldwide.

GRAPE VARIETIES AND SEEDLESS GRAPES

Grapes come in many colors, including green, red, and black. A grape's color is determined by its genes. Sometimes mutations, or changes to genes,

Structures support the grapevines as they grow.

naturally occur. These mutations can cause grapes to have different colors and tastes.

Seedless grapes are the result of a mutation. These grapes cannot reproduce. Farmers use cuttings to grow seedless varieties. They cut off part of a seedless grapevine and plant it in soil. The cutting will grow seedless grapes.

HARVEST

Different grape varieties are harvested at different times of the year. Most grapes are ready to harvest between August and October. When grapes ripen, they change color. For example, red grapes take on a purple color as they become ripe.

Grapes are usually harvested by hand. Workers walk along grapevines. They inspect bunches of grapes to make sure they are ripe and of good quality. Then they use knives to cut off the bunch.

Different varieties of grapes are grown for their varying traits.

Hand picking by trained experts can result in a higher-quality grape harvest.

US farmers began to use grape harvesting machines in the 1960s. These machines shake grapevines, causing the fruit to fall. Harvesters collect the grapes as they fall. Improvements in technology have made these machines more effective. Older machines sometimes damaged the crop. They also were unable to select grapes of high quality. Modern machines have optical sensors that allow them to sort out damaged grapes.

Machines speed up the grape-harvesting process.

USES

Some grapes are eaten fresh. These are called table grapes. In 2021, approximately 17 percent of grapes grown in the United States were table grapes.

Grapes are also used to make other food products. About 63 percent of US grapes are used to produce wine. Other grape products include juices and jellies.

Grapes can be left outdoors to dry, which turns them into raisins. This drying method is inexpensive but takes a lot of time. The grapes are also vulnerable to insects. Drying machines can produce raisins much faster, but they are expensive. Raisins make up a significant portion of the grape crop. Approximately 18 percent of US grapes are made into raisins.

Raisins are a good source of nutrients such as iron, potassium, and vitamin B6.

LETTUCE

Lettuce is a vegetable. Head lettuce, such as iceberg lettuce, is one type grown in the United States. Leaf lettuce, which includes romaine, is another variety produced in the nation. The leaves of head lettuce are closely packed together. The leaves of leaf lettuce are less tightly clustered.

Lettuce is a major crop in areas where the climate is warm enough to grow it year-round.

Romaine lettuce comes in red and green varieties.

Lettuces require six to eight hours of daily sunlight. They are frost resistant. These vegetables grow best in daytime temperatures around 73 degrees Fahrenheit (23°C). They need a lot of water. Lettuce wilts easily and becomes vulnerable to disease in dry conditions. It prefers loose, well-drained soil.

This crop grows quickly. Lettuce can be harvested within 90 days when planted in the summer. Lettuce planted in the fall and winter can take several more weeks to mature. In California and Arizona, it is possible to grow lettuce year-round. They are the top-producing states. Together, they produce more than 12 billion pounds (5.4 billion kg) of lettuce each year.

Slugs are among the pests that eat lettuce crops.

PESTS AND PESTICIDES

Aphids, beetles, and caterpillars are just some of the many pests that feed on lettuce. They can reduce harvests and spread diseases. Farmers commonly use pesticides to get rid of these pests.

However, some pesticides are toxic to people. Foods in grocery stores may have traces of pesticides. The US Environmental Protection Agency (EPA) makes sure that these pesticides don't threaten human health. The EPA regularly evaluates the pesticides used in farming, looking at any new research that has been done. Its pesticide rules and restrictions change over time.

BACTERIA

Leafy greens, including lettuce, can carry the bacteria *E. coli*. Some types of *E. coli* cause severe food poisoning. There are a few reasons why lettuce is especially likely to cause sickness from these bacteria. Lettuce grows close to the ground, where it can become contaminated with animal feces. People also typically eat lettuce raw in food such as salads. When food is

Pesticides are intended to reduce the amount of the crop that is lost due to pests.

cooked at a high temperature, bacteria is killed. People can prevent food poisoning by thoroughly washing lettuce and other produce.

HARVEST

Lettuce is typically harvested by hand. People use knives that have an angled edge to chop lettuce

Washing lettuce is one way to help prevent sickness caused by bacteria.

Harvesting lettuce by hand is common, although large farms may use machines.

at the base. They typically remove the outermost leaves of the lettuce. The lettuce is then transported to factories where it is cooled to prevent wilting. Sometimes the lettuce is packaged immediately. In other cases, it may be washed before packaging.

The bulb is part of the onion plant's stem, but it grows underground.

ONIONS

Onions are a type of vegetable. Many onion varieties are grown. Onion bulbs can be yellow, red, or white. In addition to the bulb, onion leaves and flowers are also edible. Green onions are onions that are harvested before they are fully grown.

Farmers plant onions in the spring. While the bulb is growing, onions need at least 13 hours of sunlight. Onions need to be watered often. These vegetables have shallow roots.

It is important that the soil is kept moist but is not flooded.

GROWING ONIONS

Variation in onions occurs naturally. Pollination by bees and other insects causes genes to mix. But in the 1950s, farmers began to use techniques to pollinate onions themselves. Over time, this created hybrid varieties. Farmers were able to select certain traits, such as shape and resistance to disease.

American onion farmers plant an average of 125,000 acres (51,000 ha) of onions a year.

Shovels or garden hoes can be used to lift onion bulbs out of the ground.

US farmers grow about 6.75 billion pounds (3 billion kg) of onions each year. California is the top-producing state. In 2020, the state's onion industry was valued at almost $900 million.

HARVEST

Farmers often harvest onions at night. This is because onion bulbs can be damaged if they are exposed to too much sunlight. Some onion varieties are delicate and must be harvested by hand. First a machine loosens the onions from the soil. Then workers use a tool that lifts the bulb out of the ground.

Other onion varieties are tougher and can withstand machine harvests. First, farmers use a mower to chop off the top of the plant. Then they drive a large vehicle called a wind roller over the rows of onions. The wind roller digs up the onions. A third vehicle known as a top air is responsible for sorting the bulbs from leaves, dirt, and other debris.

In factories, workers check onions to make sure they are of good quality. Onions also pass through optical sorting machines that can detect whether an onion is damaged. The damaged onions are removed. The rest are packaged and prepared for shipping.

Machines harvest the onions and drop them on the ground, where they are left to dry for a few days.

Tractor-pulled machines collect dried onions from the ground.

USES

Onions have different qualities depending on when they are harvested. Spring and summer onions have thinner skins than onions harvested in fall and winter. Spring and summer onions also tend to be sweeter and juicier.

Because of these different traits and flavors, onions are used in a range of dishes. Spring and summer onions are best raw, such as in salads or sandwiches. They can also be pickled or lightly grilled. Fall and winter onions are better suited to make caramelized onions or dishes with longer cook times.

When sautéing onions for a recipe, it is best to use low or medium heat. High heat will make them bitter.

Peach trees usually begin producing fruit two to four years after being planted.

PEACHES

Peaches are fruits that grow on trees. They come in three main varieties: yellow, white, and red. Yellow peaches are the most common type in the United States. Some fruit trees require pollen from other trees of the same type before they can produce fruit. But peach trees are self-fertile. This means a single tree is able to grow fruit by itself.

Peach trees grow best in full sunlight and slightly sandy soil. They need moderate temperatures, with summer temperatures around 75 degrees Fahrenheit (24°C). Soil should be kept moist, especially around young trees.

In 2021, the United States produced 661,890 tons (600,457 metric tons) of peaches. The peach industry brought in $624 million that year. California, South Carolina, Georgia, and New Jersey were the top peach-producing states.

PESTS

Many types of insects are pests to peach trees. The plum curculio beetle is one example. Female beetles lay their eggs within the fruit. When grubs hatch from the eggs, they eat the peaches from the inside.

Farmers can use pesticides to protect their crops. However, these chemicals should not be

One of Georgia's nicknames is the Peach State. The fruit appears on signs welcoming visitors to the state.

used within two weeks of harvest. Small or privately owned orchards may opt for fruit bags. These bags can be tied around fruit to prevent plum curculio and other pests from reaching the peaches.

HARVEST AND USES

Peaches are typically harvested from late June through August. People can tell when peaches are ripe by the color of

Farmers wear protective equipment when spraying pesticides on their peach trees.

Fresh peaches are a popular snack. One medium peach provides 11 percent of the vitamin C needed each day.

their skins. Ripe peaches are completely yellow. There should not be any green on their skins.

Peaches bruise easily, so people must carefully pick them by hand. Peaches are then taken to factories where they are cleaned, inspected for blemishes, and sealed with wax to maintain freshness.

Approximately 55 percent of peaches are processed before being sold. Most processed peaches are canned. They may also be frozen or dried. Peaches may be added to yogurts or made into beverages. The remaining 45 percent are sold fresh.

Peanuts grow well in loose, sandy soil.

PEANUTS

Peanuts are legumes, not nuts. Legumes are a type of bean. They include crops such as peas, lentils, and soybeans. Legumes produce seeds that are protected in pods. Peanut pods grow underground. The seeds inside the pod are the parts people eat. Above ground, the plant looks like a bush.

Peanuts grow best in areas with long, warm summers. These plants need full sun. They require about 1 inch (2.5 cm) of water each week. From planting to harvesting, the growing cycle of a peanut takes 130 to 160 days.

Peanuts are primarily grown in the southeastern United States. Georgia is the top producer of peanuts.

In 2022, the state accounted for more than 50 percent of the nation's peanut harvest.

HARVESTING PEANUTS

Peanut harvesting typically occurs in September and October. Each plant produces about 30 to 40 nuts. Farmers stop watering peanuts

Peanut pods grow at the ends of pegs, parts coming off the plant's branches that extend underground.

A tractor with a digger attachment is used in the first step of the peanut harvest.

about two weeks before harvest. If the soil is too wet, the plant's stems will snap during harvest. The seed pods will not come out when workers pull the stems.

Special machines are used to harvest peanuts. First, farmers drive diggers between the rows of plants. These machines

dig the peanut plants out from underground. The plants are left to dry in the sun for a few days. Later, farmers use a shaker. This machine shakes the plants, causing the dried seed pods to separate from the leafy part of the plant.

Machines scoop up peanuts from the ground.

Americans consume more than 600 million pounds (272 million kg) of peanuts each year.

USES

Peanuts are used in a variety of foods. About 60 percent of the peanuts grown in the United States become peanut butter. Peanut shells are removed to make this product. A machine called a grinder crushes the seeds into small pieces. Peanuts are ground until they have a creamy texture. Ingredients such as salt, sugar, and oil are added.

Some peanuts are sold as snack foods. They may be roasted. Some are coated in honey or other flavorful ingredients. About 15 percent of peanuts are used to produce peanut oil.

Modern peanut butter was invented in the late 1800s. Since then, it has become a massively popular spread in the United States.

POTATOES

Potatoes are starchy vegetables. The edible parts of the potato plant grow underground. The rest of the plant is poisonous. If a potato spud has sprouted, it contains these poisons and should not be eaten.

Potatoes need at least six hours of direct sunlight each day. They grow best at temperatures between 61 and 66 degrees Fahrenheit (16 and 19°C).

From above the ground, potatoes may look like simple leafy plants.

In Idaho, farmers grow potatoes within view of the scenic Teton mountain range.

However, potatoes can survive a light frost. They need about 2 inches (5 cm) of water each week.

Potatoes are the most commonly grown vegetables on US farms. More than 200 types of potatoes are grown in the United States. These include many types of russet potatoes, red potatoes, and white potatoes. Idaho and Washington State are the top potato-growing states.

PESTS AND DISEASES

Potatoes are vulnerable to pests such as the Colorado potato beetle. Both adult beetles and their young eat potato leaves. They can kill the plants and cause extreme damage to potato crops.

Farmers may use pesticides to kill insects and prevent them from eating their crops. But the Colorado potato beetle has developed resistance to many pesticides. This means the pesticides no longer harm these beetles. It can be difficult to limit damage if an infestation occurs.

Plant diseases, such as blight, also affect potato crops. Blight causes openings to appear on potato tubers. Bacteria can grow in these openings, causing the potatoes to rot.

The Colorado potato beetle is a major threat to potato crops.

Machines help farmers harvest potatoes and load them for transport.

Scientists are working to develop a GMO potato that would be less vulnerable to blight. Genetic changes have already been made to some potatoes. White russet potatoes are genetically modified to prevent browning after the vegetable has been cut.

HARVEST AND USES

It takes about five months for potatoes to grow. When the crop is ready to harvest, its leaves turn yellow. This occurs in late summer, from August to September.

Potatoes may bruise during harvest. To prevent bruising, farmers must pay attention to soil moisture and soil temperature. Potatoes should be harvested when the soil is moist, but not completely wet. If the soil conditions are not correct, the potatoes can get damaged during the harvest.

Potatoes are fat-free and low in sodium. One medium potato provides 30 percent of the vitamin C needed daily.

Potatoes should be harvested when soil temperatures are 50 degrees Fahrenheit (10°C) or warmer.

Farmers use harvesters to dig up potatoes. The vegetables are loaded onto trucks and taken to processing facilities. Sometimes processing is minimal. Potatoes can be sold fresh. Fresh potatoes can be baked or mashed.

Other potato products require more processing. For example, French fries are made from potatoes. To make frozen fries, potatoes are cleaned and peeled in factories. They are cut into shape. The fries are washed to remove loose starches. This step helps ensure that fries are an even golden-brown color when they are fried. Next, the fries are boiled. This gets rid of sugars in the potato and gives fries their texture. Finally, the fries are partially dried using hot air. The fries are frozen, packaged, and sent to stores.

Potatoes can also be made into chips. The potatoes are cleaned and peeled. Then a machine with sharp blades cuts the potatoes into thin slices. The slices are washed to remove excess starches. Next, the potato slices are fried in extremely hot oil. Water within the potato slices boils out and is replaced with the oil, giving the chips their crispy texture. Once the chips have been thoroughly cooked, they are seasoned with salt and other flavors.

Processing plants transform truckloads of potatoes into potato chips.

RICE

Rice is a grain. It grows on a type of grass. Flowers bloom on the grass. Wind pollinates these flowers, which leads to the development of seeds. The seeds are the parts of rice plants that people eat.

Rice is one of the world's most important food crops. More than half of the world's population relies on rice as a food source.

Processing is required before people can eat the seeds of the rice plant.

More than 120,000 varieties of rice are grown worldwide. They differ in characteristics such as grain size and flavor. Black japonica rice, jasmine rice, and basmati rice are some examples of rice grown in the United States. Wild rice, which is grown mostly in Minnesota and California, grows on a different species of grass. Scientists classify it separately from the more common type of rice.

Rice planting lasts from February to May. Rice is a semiaquatic plant that needs a lot of water. Because of this, rice grows best in loamy soils that hold water well. During the growing season, rice fields remain flooded with 2 to 4 inches (5 to 10 cm) of water. This crop grows best in hot, humid climates with a lot of sunlight.

Farmers flood their rice fields during the growing season.

RICE IN THE UNITED STATES

The United States produces approximately 20 billion pounds (9.1 billion kg) of rice each year. The rice industry brings in about $34 billion annually to the US economy. Arkansas is the top producer of rice in the United States, accounting for more than 40 percent of the harvest.

Rice production has fallen in the 2020s. Climate change is one reason for this reduction. Climate change has led to frequent droughts, which make it challenging and costly to grow rice. The changing climate also causes temperatures to become more extreme. At high temperatures, rice plants produce fewer seeds.

The intense water requirements for rice make the crop especially challenging to grow during droughts.

HARVEST AND USES

Rice harvests take place from mid-July to November. When it is time for harvest, water is drained from rice fields. Farmers drive combines through the fields. These machines cut the grasses and separate the seeds from the rest of the plant. The rice grains are transported to facilities where they are dried with hot air.

Combines harvest multiple rows of rice at a time.

Milling is the next step in processing rice. When rice seeds are harvested, they have three layers: the hull, the bran, and the endosperm. They also have an oily section at the base of the seed known as the germ. The hull is the outermost layer. Humans cannot digest this layer, so it is removed during the milling process. Rice seeds that still have their hulls are called paddy rice. They are used as animal feed. After the hulls have been removed, the rice can be sold for human consumption.

The bran is underneath the hull. This part of the seed gives rice its color. It may be brown, black, or red. Rice seeds can be milled further to remove the bran and the germ. This is how white rice is made. Machines rub away the bran and germ so that only the white endosperm remains.

Rice is used in many dishes, including sushi and burritos. It can be added to curries and made into risotto. Rice flour is gluten-free and can be used to make noodles and pastries.

Paddy rice, *left*, is used as animal feed and white rice, *right*, is used in human foods.

SOYBEANS

Soybeans are legumes. This crop needs at least eight hours of sunlight every day. It grows best at temperatures around 70 degrees Fahrenheit (21°C). Soybeans should be watered regularly. In the early stages of growth, soybeans need about 0.7 inches (1.8 cm) of water per week. The plants need about twice as much water when they are flowering and growing pods.

Soybean plants can produce more than 200 soybeans each.

The pods of the soybean plant typically contain three soybeans.

GROWING SOYBEANS

In 2022, the soybean industry brought in more than $34 billion to the United States. The country is one of the largest producers of soybeans in the world. Illinois was the top-producing soybean state in 2022. Other major producers of soybeans include Iowa and Minnesota.

Combines harvest the soybeans and transfer them to another vehicle for transport.

HARVEST AND USES

The seed pods of soybeans turn yellow when they are mature. But in most cases, harvest does not occur until the pods have dried out and become brown. This typically takes place beginning in mid-October. Farmers use combines to cut the soybean plants and separate the pods from the stems. The pods are taken to facilities where they are stored and processed.

Soybeans can be harvested before the pods reach maturity. When the pods are green and juicy, they can be eaten fresh. As a food crop, soybeans have many uses. Soybean sprouts can be added to salads and other dishes. Soybeans can be made into tofu. Dried soybeans are boiled, roasted, and ground up to make soy flour. This flour can be used to make soy milk. Soy sauce is another food product made from soybeans.

Tofu, soy milk, and soy sauce are among the many food products made from soybeans.

SQUASH

Many crops are classified as squash. All squash are fruits. Some types of squash are summer crops, such as yellow squash and zucchini. Other squash crops are harvested in the fall, including pumpkin and butternut squash. These crops are called winter squash because they can be stored and eaten throughout the winter.

Squash, such as pumpkins, are grown in areas commonly called patches.

Zucchini and yellow squash produce long, tubular fruits.

Summer and winter squash should be planted after the last frost. They need full sunlight and warm temperatures. Both types of squash need about 1 to 2 inches (2.5 to 5 cm) of water each week. They should be watered slowly at the base of the plant so that the water can fully seep into the soil.

GROWING SQUASH

In 2021, the United States produced more than 690 million pounds (313 million kg) of squash. By weight, Michigan was the top-producing state. It grew 23 percent of US squash that year.

Summer squash are vulnerable to a disease called zucchini yellow mosaic virus (ZYMV). It is spread by aphids and affects all kinds of squash. Infected squash are discolored and do not

Butternut squash is a popular choice for autumn recipes. It provides nutrients such as calcium. It also provides more than 100 percent of the vitamin A needed each day.

grow to full size. Their skins may have a warty texture. The infected squash rots more quickly than healthy squash.

Scientists created a GMO summer squash that is resistant to ZYMV. The US Food and Drug Administration (FDA) approved the growing and selling of this GMO crop in 1995. It was one of the first GMO crops sold in the United States. This GMO crop helps prevent food waste by reducing the amount of infected or rotten squash that needs to be thrown away. The majority of summer squash grown in the country is not genetically modified.

HARVEST AND USES

Winter squash tend to be larger and grow slower than summer squash. Winter squash are harvested when the fruit reaches maturity. Summer squash are harvested when the fruit is still immature. This is why winter squash tends to have thicker rinds than summer squash.

Yellowed leaves are one visible symptom of ZYMV.

Zucchini harvesting is done by hand.

Summer squash are cut from plants by hand. A small piece of the stem remains on the squash. The fruit is delicate and needs to be handled carefully to prevent scarring. Because summer squash does not store well, these squash are sold quickly after harvest. They are harvested about three times a week during the harvest season.

Unlike summer squash, winter squash can be stored for several months. At harvest, the rinds of winter squash should be tough enough that they cannot be broken open with a fingernail. Winter squash are harvested once or twice during a season.

Squash are sold fresh and can be eaten in many ways. Some types, such as zucchini, can be eaten raw. Others are prepared by frying, roasting, or steaming. They can be used in soups or processed into substitutes for pasta.

Pumpkin pie, made using the flesh of small pumpkins, is a classic autumn treat.

STRAWBERRIES

In order to produce the best fruit, strawberry plants should receive eight or more hours of sunlight a day. They need 1 to 1.5 inches (2.5 to 3.8 cm) of water each week. Many strawberry varieties exist. Some types grow more quickly than others. Strawberries also differ in size, flavor, and color.

Farmers should follow expert guidelines for spacing their strawberry crops. This gives the plants enough room to grow and develop.

Most states can grow strawberries for only five months of the year. But in California, strawberries are grown and sold year-round. The state produces more than 91 percent of the strawberries grown in the United States.

Slugs are among the pests that can harm strawberry crops.

PESTS AND GENE MODIFICATIONS

Many types of insects and other pests eat strawberry plants. Farmers may use pesticides to stop these pests. But some pesticides are toxic to people. In 2022, researchers analyzed 46 types of fruits and vegetables. They found that strawberries were the fruit most likely to be contaminated by pesticides.

Pests are not the only challenge that strawberry farmers must handle. Strawberries have a short shelf life, meaning they can rot quickly. This can lead to food waste if farmers grow more strawberries than they can sell.

Scientists hope that genetic modifications can extend the shelf life of strawberries. They will use gene editing. This means scientists will turn existing characteristics on and off. Genes are naturally turned on and off through breeding, but gene editing is a quicker way to get desired traits.

Picking the fruit by hand helps protect the delicate strawberries.

HARVEST AND USES

Strawberries are harvested at different times in different places. In southern states, harvests occur around April and May. In northern states, harvests may not begin until late June.

Strawberries bruise easily, so they must be picked by hand. Looking at a strawberry's color helps determine its ripeness. A ripe strawberry is shiny and red.

Most strawberries grown in the United States are sold fresh. But strawberries can also be frozen or dried. They can be made into other food products, such as syrups and jams.

Strawberries are sometimes dipped in chocolate and enjoyed as a dessert.

SUGARCANE

Sugarcane is a type of tall grass. It has thin leaves and a thick stem with joints. Like other grasses, sugarcane continues growing after it has been cut.

Sugarcane can grow more than 10 feet (3 m) tall.

All plants use the sun's energy to create sugar. Farmers grow sugarcane for the crop's ability to store sugar in its stem. The sugar the plant naturally produces can be processed to make cane sugar and other products.

Sugarcane originally grew in areas with tropical climates. Because of this, the crop grows in hot temperatures between 90 and 100 degrees Fahrenheit (32 and 38°C). Temperatures should be cooler during harvest, around 55 degrees Fahrenheit (13°C). Sugarcane requires full sun and frequent watering. It needs about 2 inches (5 cm) of water each week, and the surrounding soil should be kept moist.

Sugar is found within the sugarcane's thick stem.

GROWING SUGARCANE

Sugarcane accounts for approximately 45 percent of the sugar produced in the United States. Florida leads the United States in sugarcane production. Sugarcane is also commercially grown in Louisiana and Texas.

Harvesting sugarcane by hand can be difficult and time-consuming.

HARVEST

Sugarcane takes a long time to mature. In the warmest parts of the United States, planting usually occurs in the late summer or early fall. Since these regions do not experience frosts that kill sugarcane, the plant grows throughout the winter. The crop will be ready for its first harvest about a year after it was planted.

Sugarcane is often harvested by hand, though mechanical methods are gaining popularity. In hand harvesting, a machete is used to chop down the plant at the base of its stem. Next, workers put on gloves to pluck sharp leaves from the stem. Sugarcane will regrow after it is cut, but it will produce less and less sugar each time. After five or six years, the old crop is typically uprooted and new sugarcane is planted.

Using machines increases the speed and efficiency of the sugarcane harvest.

SUGAR PROCESSING

Sugar within the stem can diminish rapidly after harvest. The crop is quickly transported to mills for processing. Transforming sugarcane into sugar involves several steps. First, the sugarcane

US facilities produce millions of tons of sugar each year.

Many processing steps are needed to turn raw sugarcane into the sugar found on store shelves.

is ground up to squeeze out its sweet juices. Next, the juices are brought to a boil. They thicken into a syrup and crystalize. Spinning the crystalized substance at high speeds creates raw sugar. Raw sugar is light brown and has larger crystals than cane sugar.

To make cane sugar, raw sugar is further processed at a refinery. The raw sugar is washed and filtered to remove impurities. When the sugar crystals dry, they are white and much smaller.

Tomato plants require support to help hold their heavy fruit.

TOMATOES

People often think of tomatoes as vegetables. However, tomatoes are actually fruits. Like other fruits, tomatoes have seeds. All fruits, including tomatoes, develop from pollinated flowers.

Tomatoes need six to eight hours of sunlight each day. They should be watered frequently. Tomatoes thrive when planted in loamy soils.

Tomatoes can be grown in every US state, and 20 states produce tomatoes commercially. The United States is one of the world's leading producers of tomatoes. Together, Florida and California grow approximately 67 percent of the nation's tomato crop.

BREEDING AND GMOs

More than 10,000 tomato varieties are grown. These varieties were created through breeding, which can take several years. Breeders pollinate plants that have the desired characteristics. After several generations, a new tomato variety is established.

Genetic modifications are another way to develop new tomato varieties. In 1994, the first GMO tomato reached grocery stores. It was called the Flavr Savr tomato. Scientists turned off a gene that causes tomatoes to become squishy as they ripen. The Flavr Savr tomato could stay fresh longer than other tomatoes.

Tomato varieties come in many shapes and sizes.

In 2022, the USDA approved a purple GMO tomato. The tomato is purple because it is rich in antioxidants, which are substances with potential health benefits. Snapdragon plants have genes that cause them to produce antioxidants. These genes were added to a tomato's genes. In addition to its health benefits, scientists expect the purple tomato to have a longer shelf life than other types of tomatoes.

Tomato harvesters can quickly process thousands of tomatoes.

HARVEST AND USES

Farmers use harvesters to pick tomatoes. These machines also sort out soil and other debris from the crop. A color-sorting machine gets rid of tomatoes that are discolored. Workers do additional sorting at the back of the machine. They get rid of any discolored or damaged tomatoes that the machine missed.

Approximately 8 percent of US tomatoes are sold fresh. Tomatoes are also processed to make products. They may be canned or made into sauce or juice. Ketchup is a mixture of tomato paste, water, sugar, salt, vinegar, and other seasonings.

Tomato juice is a good source of vitamin C, vitamin A, and other important nutrients.

Watermelons need warmth, sun, and space to grow successfully.

WATERMELONS

Watermelons are large fruits. They grow on sprawling vines and need lots of space. Each plant requires about 20 square feet (1.9 sq m) to grow. Adding fertilizer to loamy soils before planting can help produce larger fruit. Watermelons grow best in warm temperatures. They need eight hours of full sun every day and about 1 to 2 inches (2.5 to 5 cm) of water each week.

In 2021, the United States produced 3.4 billion pounds (1.5 billion kg) of watermelons. This crop is primarily grown in southern states with warm climates. In 2021, Florida

and Georgia were the top-producing states. In the 2010s, the worldwide demand for seedless watermelons increased, and Florida increased its seedless watermelon production. Seedless watermelons are more expensive and harder to grow, so they are sold at higher prices.

Shoppers can pay more for the convenience of a seedless watermelon, *left*.

HARVEST AND USES

Each watermelon plant produces two to three fruits. Watermelons are harvested when the fruit reaches maturity. The fruit does not ripen after the harvest.

Watermelons are harvested by hand. Workers use a knife to cut watermelons from the vine. They flip these watermelons over to let other workers know that the fruit is ready to

Harvesting watermelons is a labor-intensive process.

People often enjoy juicy watermelons at summer barbecues. Watermelons are the top-selling melon in the United States.

be collected. The outside of a watermelon is mostly green. But the part that touches the ground is a yellow color because it didn't receive any sunlight.

Other workers load the watermelons onto trucks to be transported to factories. There, people inspect the fruits for damage and wash them. Then the watermelons are packaged and sold fresh.

Farmers have been growing wheat for more than 10,000 years.

WHEAT

Wheat is a type of grass grown for its edible grains. The crop can be made into flour. Wheat is grouped into six classes that vary in color and hardness. Each class of wheat produces flour with different qualities. The different flours are each suited to different foods.

GROWING WHEAT

Wheat can be planted in spring or fall, depending on the climate. In places with cold winters and rainy summers, wheat is planted in spring. In areas with

mild winters and drier summers, farmers plant wheat in the fall.

Wheat can endure a wide range of temperatures. It will grow at temperatures between 40 and 95 degrees Fahrenheit (4 and 35°C). The crop does not need much water. It needs just 12 to 15 inches (30 to 38 cm) of water over the entire growing season. It grows best in loamy soils.

Tractor attachments help farmers quickly plant wheat fields when the time is right.

Wheat fields cover more than 78,000 square miles (202,000 sq km) of US land. Wheat is commercially grown in 42 states. In 2020, North Dakota and Kansas were the leading wheat producers in the United States. In 2022, the US wheat industry was worth $14.6 billion, making wheat one of the most valuable crops in the country.

Farms may use multiple combines to harvest large wheat fields more quickly.

Combines are major investments for farmers. These machines can cost hundreds of thousands of dollars.

HARVEST

Farmers use combines to harvest wheat. These machines perform several steps. They cut the wheat at the stem and sort the grains from the other plant material. A tractor pulling a grain cart typically drives alongside the combine. An unloading auger on the combine transfers the sorted grains into the grain cart.

MILLING AND FOOD PRODUCTS

The wheat grain is encased in a hull. Another layer called the bran lies beneath the hull. Wheat can be easily shaken out of its hull. To make some food products, such as white flour, the bran must be removed during the milling process.

Milling wheat creates flour. Additional sorting occurs at flour mills to ensure that only wheat kernels are milled. Then the kernels are soaked in water. This makes it easier to remove the bran in later steps. Next, a grinding machine crushes the kernels. The crushed pieces are sifted, which separates the bran

Wheat requires significant processing to reach its commonly eaten forms.

Bread is among the most popular food products made from wheat.

from the inner part of the wheat kernel. This process of grinding and sifting is repeated several times until the particles are very fine. Both the bran and the inner kernel can be made into types of flour.

Many food products are made using wheat. Pasta, cereals, and breads can all be made from wheat flour. Wheat flour can also be used to make bagels, crackers, and cakes.

FEED CROPS

Alfalfa is also known as lucerne.

ALFALFA

Alfalfa is a legume. It is related to crops such as peas, beans, and peanuts. Alfalfa plants can grow to be about 3 feet (0.9 m) tall. They have a central stem that branches into a leafy crown.

Alfalfa is a perennial plant. It is primarily grown as a feed crop. It also improves soil health. The plant is relatively easy to grow and can survive in poor soil. It sprouts in seven to ten days. Alfalfa is resistant to drought and needs less than 2 inches (5 cm) of water per week. Alfalfa should be planted in full sun.

GROWING ALFALFA

Alfalfa is primarily grown in the western United States. In 2019, Montana grew 2.1 million acres (850,000 ha) of alfalfa hay, the most of any US state. California and Idaho are other top producers.

The alfalfa plant grows purple flowers.

In 2011, a GMO alfalfa crop was approved by the USDA. The GMO crop was created to be resistant to herbicides, which are chemicals used to kill weeds. Weeds compete with alfalfa for nutrients. Spraying herbicides that kill weeds but do not affect alfalfa increases harvests. GMO alfalfa is safe for livestock to eat.

Alfalfa is a major crop in the United States.

Dried alfalfa is turned into bales of hay so it can be sold as livestock feed.

NUTRITION

When alfalfa is grown for livestock, it is harvested before it flowers. Alfalfa is easier for animals to digest in the early stages of growth. After alfalfa is cut, the harvest is dried to make hay.

Alfalfa hay is mainly fed to dairy cows. But other livestock, including horses, beef cows, and sheep, can eat alfalfa. Alfalfa is rich in fiber, which can improve gut health. The crop also supplies other important nutrients such as protein, minerals, and vitamins.

Barley was the main grain used for making bread in ancient Greece and ancient Rome.

BARLEY

Barley is a grain. It was the first grain people grew for agricultural purposes. It originated near present-day Egypt and is now grown all over the world.

Barley is a grass with a long stem and a few leaves. It has flowers that produce kernels. Each plant produces between 20 and 60 kernels.

Barley needs at least six hours of sunlight each day. Its soil should be kept moist, but it is important not to overwater it. Barley plants grow best in well-drained, loamy soils. Depending on the climate, barley can be planted in the spring and the fall. The spring variety is more common in the United States. Northern states and places with cold winters can grow only the spring variety, as the crop will not survive the winter temperatures.

BARLEY IN THE UNITED STATES

In 2021, Idaho and Montana grew 57 percent of US barley. Barley planted in the spring is harvested in late summer. Farmers use combines to harvest barley. These vehicles cut and gather the barley. Then blades in the machine thresh the barley, or separate the edible parts from the husk and straw. Combines also remove barley seeds from their shells.

Barley contains little gluten compared with wheat.

Like other grains, barley kernels have several layers. These layers may be stripped off as barley is processed. Whole grain barley has the outermost layer, or the hull, removed. Barley without the hull is preferred for livestock. Pot barley and pearl barley have more layers removed.

About 75 percent of barley grown in the United States is malted. During this process, barley is soaked in water and then dried with hot air. This process changes starches in the barley into sugar. The resulting product is called malt. Relatively little barley is directly eaten by people. But malt is used to make many food products, including bagels, milkshakes, beer, and candies.

Combines perform the initial steps of processing as they harvest barley.

A machine called a kiln helps dry barley as part of the malting process.

Farmers add grain to hay when feeding livestock.

BARLEY FEED

Livestock feed is another major use of barley, accounting for 21 percent of barley harvests. Many types of farm animals eat barley, including horses and sheep. Barley is often fed to beef cattle to help them grow quickly.

Barley has a higher protein content than corn. However, it lacks some nutrients that are present in corn-based animal feed. For this reason, barley is often used to supplement an animal's diet.

Whole grain barley can be stored in airtight containers for up to two years. Heat and moisture can cause mold to grow on barley. Barley that has a foul odor should be disposed of and not fed to livestock. Insects and other pests can also get into stored barley. Barley should be thrown out if an infestation occurs.

Farmers monitor their stored barley carefully to make sure it stays dry, cool, and fresh.

CLOVER

Clover is a type of legume. It can be planted for ground cover or to hold soil in place. Clover adds nutrients to the soil as it grows. Nectar from clover can serve as food for honeybees. The bees use this nectar to produce clover honey, which is prized by beekeepers for its flowery flavor. Farmers also plant clover to provide food for livestock.

Pollinators such as butterflies, moths, and honeybees are attracted to clover flowers.

A four-leaf clover is the symbol of 4-H, a network of agricultural youth organizations.

Farmers prepare the soil before planting clover. This crop is sensitive to herbicides, so weeds must be eliminated before clover crops are planted. Agricultural lime, which is crushed limestone or chalk, can also be added to soil to encourage clover growth.

Clover can be grown in full or partial sun. It needs two to six hours of sunlight every day. Clover can grow in slightly dry conditions but thrives when the soil is kept moist. It needs about 45 inches (114 cm) of water during the growing season. Farmers must not overwater clover, as it cannot survive in standing water.

Cutting clover can be done with a relatively small tractor.

HARVEST

Clover is harvested for its seeds. Annual and perennial clover are harvested the same way. A harvesting machine cuts the crop and gathers the cut clover into rows. The crop is left to dry for about a week.

Combines are used during the next stage of the harvest. A pickup head is attached to the combine to easily gather the clover. The combine separates the seeds from the rest of the crop. The seeds are taken to cleaning facilities where remaining weeds and dirt are removed.

NUTRITION

Not all clover is harvested. Livestock, such as sheep and cattle, can graze on certain varieties of clover. These crops are rich in protein. Studies have shown that cattle that feed on clover put on weight more quickly.

However, farmers must be careful not to feed their livestock too much clover. The crop can cause bloating if eaten in large amounts. Clover can be harvested and stored as hay for livestock to feed on during the winter. However, a toxic mold can grow on stored clover. Livestock that eat this mold stop producing vitamin K. This can be deadly for the livestock. Certain clover, such as the alsike clover, are also toxic to livestock. Farmers must be aware of which kind of clover they are feeding to their animals.

Clover is a highly nutritious crop for feeding livestock.

Each kernel of field corn has a small dent at the top.

CORN

Field corn is the main type of corn used to feed livestock. It has hard yellow kernels. The kernels appear dented when dry, so field corn is also called dent corn. Field corn does not have a sweet taste. It has a starchy texture.

Field corn is often used to supplement the diets of pigs and cattle. It is high in nutrients such as carbohydrates, fats, and proteins. Adding corn to the diet of these animals helps them grow quickly.

CORN FACTS

The United States is the world's largest producer of corn. Approximately 90 million acres (36 million ha) of corn is grown in the United States each year. Field corn accounts for 99 percent of US corn production.

HARVEST

In most states, corn harvesting begins in September. People can tell if corn is ready for harvest by looking at the silk. The silk should be brown and dry.

Field corn is typically harvested using a combine. The machine strips the dry kernels from the cob. Unlike with sweet corn, farmers are not concerned about the kernels losing moisture during the harvest.

Corn is a source of carbohydrates and protein, which provide chickens with energy to grow.

HAY

Hay is made of a variety of dried plants. Hayseed often includes alfalfa, clover, and timothy grass. These plants are harvested and dried to produce hay.

Many plants that are used to make hay are perennials. They do not need to be replanted each year. Hay should be planted in fields that do not have many weeds. Weeds compete with hay crops for nutrients. Herbicides that kill weeds will also

The round shape of some hay bales makes them more resistant to moisture than square bales.

Hay is made into round or square bales.

harm the crop. For high-quality hay, seeds should be planted in nitrogen-rich soils. Legumes like alfalfa add this nutrient to the soil, so they are often included in hayseed mixtures.

In 2020, Texas produced the most hay of any US state. Missouri and Nebraska were other top producers. The United States has seen declines in hay production throughout the 2000s. Climate change has made droughts more common and long-lasting. In 2022, the United States produced 112.8 million tons (102.3 million metric tons) of hay. This was the lowest amount of the century so far. That year, Texas and other hay-producing states experienced severe droughts.

HARVEST AND STORAGE

People often confuse hay and straw. Both are dried plant material. However, they are harvested at different stages of plant growth. Hay is typically harvested when the crops begin to bloom. At this time, hay has the highest nutritional value. Straw is harvested after plants reach maturity. Few nutrients are left, since the crop has used them to produce seeds. Straw is mainly used as animal bedding.

Straw may look similar to hay, but it serves a different purpose.

Baling machines compress the hay into tight, dense bales.

Hay can be harvested two or three times each year. Harvesting hay involves three steps. First, farmers use mowers to cut the hay. After the hay is cut, it is left out to dry. This takes about three days of warm, sunny weather. Baling is the final step. Farmers roll the dried hay into large bales using baling machines. These machines can produce hay bales that weigh 700 pounds (318 kg). Hay bales are easier to transport and store than loose hay.

During harvest, it is important for hay to be kept dry. If cut hay gets wet, nutrients and vitamins will wash out. The hay will not be able to give livestock as much energy.

It is important for hay to be stored in a ventilated area.

Hay can be stored outdoors or in a barn. However, it is best to keep hay in areas that are well ventilated and dry. These conditions make mold less likely to grow. Moldy hay should not be fed to livestock, as it can make animals sick.

NUTRITION

Hay is primarily produced as livestock feed. Horses, cattle, sheep, and many other animals can eat hay. Pets such as rabbits also eat it. The crop is often given as feed to livestock during winter or times of drought, when other food sources are scarce.

Harvested hay has similar protein and mineral levels compared with hay that is growing in pastures. But cut hay loses vitamins and fats over time. It is important to supplement livestock diets with other feeds to ensure that animals are getting the nutrients they need.

Hay can be given to livestock using a feeding rack.

Oat crops are used to make both feed and straw.

OATS

Oats are a type of grass. When oat grasses are fully grown, they can be more than 4 feet (1.2 m) tall. The grasses have hanging structures that each contain an oat. The oat is protected by an outer hull.

Several varieties of oats are grown. Some are planted in the spring, while others are planted in the fall. Oats that are planted in the fall begin to germinate, or develop, before winter begins. Once cold weather arrives, the seeds become dormant and stop growing. They begin growing again when spring arrives and temperatures get warmer.

Oats grow in cool, moist conditions. They struggle in hot, dry weather. Because oats require cool temperatures, they are mainly grown in the upper Midwest. South Dakota and

Minnesota are the primary growers of oats in the United States. Together, they produce about one-third of US oats.

Compared with wheat and barley, oats are less likely to be harmed by insects. The crop's roots also produce chemicals

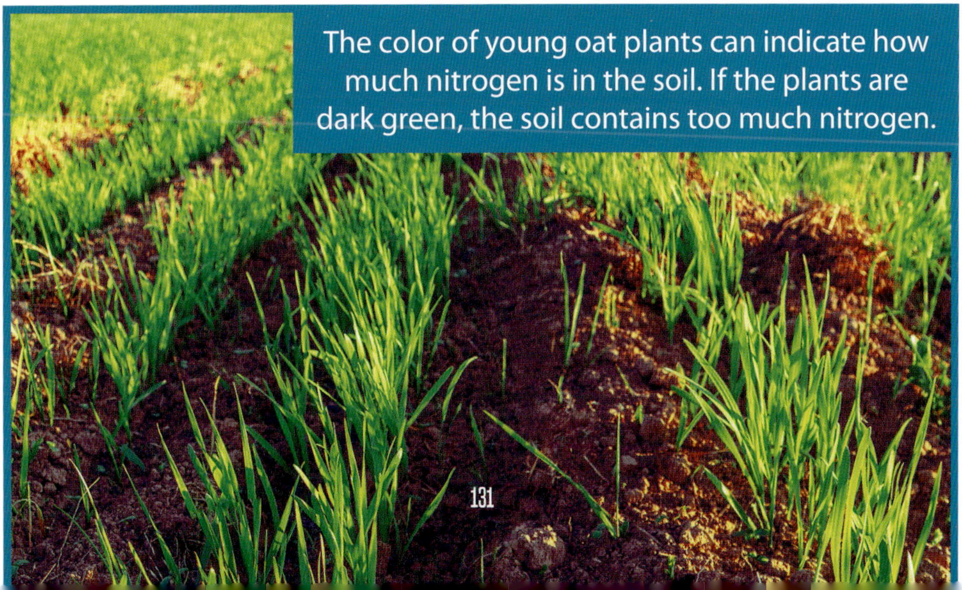

The color of young oat plants can indicate how much nitrogen is in the soil. If the plants are dark green, the soil contains too much nitrogen.

that limit weed growth near the plant. However, oats and other grasses are vulnerable to a plant disease called rust. Rust is caused by a fungus. Infected plants have yellow, orange, or red spots on their leaves.

HARVEST AND PROCESSING

The timing of the oat harvest depends on the variety planted. Combines are typically used to harvest oats. These machines cut the grass and separate the stems from the oats.

Rust affects oats, wheat, barley, and many other plants.

Oats with hulls look different from the oatmeal people are familiar with.

Oats are then taken to mills for processing. First, the oats go through machines that sort out unwanted materials such as straw. Then hulling machines remove the tough outer layer, or hull, of each oat. Oat hulls are used in animal feed. The soft innards of the oat may be processed further. They may be roasted in kilns and crushed. This part of the oat is used in foods that people eat.

Oats may be fed to livestock as part of a mixture with other types of feed.

USES

Oats are primarily used in animal feed. They are full of nutrients. Once oats were the primary food for cattle. The crop has high levels of protein, which helps cattle grow. Today cows are raised mostly on corn diets. But some research shows that an oat-based diet has health benefits. Farmers have reported that cows that are fed oats have lower levels of cholesterol than other cattle.

Oats are high in fat. They provide an energy boost, which makes them a good option for horses. Oats are even used in food for dogs and cats.

For people, oats are used to make foods such as oatmeal and granola bars. They can also be processed to make oat flour and oat milk. Eating oats can improve health. It can lower cholesterol and blood sugar levels.

Oat milk has become a popular alternative to cow's milk.

Sorghum can be grown in multiple color varieties.

SORGHUM

Sorghum is a grain plant. Sorghum plants produce small clusters of flowers about 55 days after they sprout. Pollinated flowers produce kernels. A cluster of sorghum flowers may contain as many as 3,000 kernels.

Sorghum needs full sun to grow. The crop can grow in hot temperatures and tolerate drought conditions. It is able to grow in slightly sandy soils. Sorghum needs about 4 inches (10 cm) of water every ten days.

The United States is the world's leading producer of sorghum. The crop grows in 21 states. In 2021, Kansas and Texas grew nearly 75 percent of US sorghum.

HARVEST AND STORAGE

Sorghum is ready to harvest after about 90 days. In some climates, it can be harvested multiple times throughout the year. The crop is mature when the kernels have dark spots. By this time, the moisture levels in the plant have decreased.

The ideal moisture level for sorghum at harvest time is 20 percent.

Farmers use combines to harvest sorghum. Combines cut sorghum stalks and separate the grain heads from the rest of the plant. The grains are dried in industrial driers.

Drying sorghum is necessary for proper storage. Sorghum should be stored in areas with good ventilation. This helps prevent moisture buildup that can lead to mold growth. It also limits pests. Farmers should inspect stored sorghum once a week to make sure there is no excess moisture. They can run fans to help keep sorghum dry.

Traditional outdoor methods of sorghum drying can leave the grain vulnerable to wildlife.

Sorghum is a good energy source for some farm animals.

NUTRITION AND OTHER USES

Sorghum has high amounts of carbohydrates. It also is rich in fiber. However, sorghum has less nutritional content than corn. Sorghum is primarily fed to chickens and pigs, but other animals can also digest sorghum.

Sorghum has other uses in addition to livestock feed. It can be made into syrup and woven materials, such as mats and baskets. Sugars from the crop can also be used to produce ethanol. Ethanol is a chemical used in many products, including cosmetics, medicines, plastics, and fuel.

SOYBEANS

More than 70 percent of soybeans grown in the United States are used as feed for animals. They are processed into a form called soybean meal. Poultry, pigs, and cows are the main animals that eat soybean meal. But other livestock, including horses and fish, also eat soybeans.

Livestock farmers need to carefully store soybean meal so the feed does not rot or get eaten by insects. Soybeans should be stored in cool, dry spaces to reduce the risk of mold and pests. In ideal conditions, processed soybeans can be stored for 18 months and remain safe for animals to eat.

Soybean meal is the most widely used source of protein for livestock.

The first US GMO soybeans were introduced in 1996. Known as Roundup Ready, they were created to resist the popular herbicide Roundup.

NUTRITION

Soybeans are rich in protein and fat. They are one of the cheapest forms of protein on the market. A 2019 study from Kansas State University found that pigs that were fed soybean meal had more energy than pigs that were fed cornmeal. Soybeans also have nutrients that lead to muscle growth.

It is important that livestock eat a varied diet. Eating too many soybeans can harm gut health in cattle. Poultry may suffer from a lack of certain vitamins if they are fed only soybeans. The lack of these vitamins can lead to diseases.

GMO

In 2020, approximately 94 percent of US soybeans were GMOs. Most GMO soy is used for animal feed. These plants are modified to be more resistant to herbicides.

FIBER CROPS

A cotton plant's bolls appear and mature only after the plant's flowering stage.

COTTON

Cotton plants are a type of woody shrub. These plants typically grow to between 3.2 and 6.6 feet (1 and 2 m) tall. They flower approximately 80 days after sprouting. Pollinators help these plants produce seeds. After a few days of blooming, the flowers fall off and pods begin to develop. These pods are called bolls. Cotton bolls produce fibers that surround the plant's seeds. As the plant matures, the bolls open up and expose white fibers. These fibers can be collected and made into textiles.

Cotton plants grow best in warm weather and full sun. Fertilizers should be added to the soil to ensure a high-quality crop. While the plants are growing, they need a lot of water.

Less water is needed once the bolls develop, and cotton harvests should occur in dry conditions. The high amount of water used to grow cotton means the plant has a greater impact on the environment than many other crops.

Each cotton plant needs about 10 gallons (38 L) of water during the growing season.

US COTTON INDUSTRY

Between August 2019 and July 2020, the United States produced almost 20 million bales of cotton. A single cotton bale can produce 1,200 T-shirts. US cotton is grown primarily in the South. The seventeen states that commercially produce the crop make up the Cotton Belt. Texas grows the most cotton of any US state, accounting for about 40 percent of cotton harvests.

Large farms compress cotton into big, heavy bales. The average bale weighs 491 pounds (223 kg).

The boll weevil has long been a threat to US cotton crops.

PESTS

Cotton is vulnerable to many types of pests, including cutworms and aphids. However, a major pest known as the boll weevil has been eliminated in all US states except for Texas. The boll weevil is native to Mexico and entered the United States in the late 1800s. These beetles devasted cotton crops throughout much of the 1900s. They destroyed about 8 percent of US cotton each year, causing many cotton farms to go out of business. In total, boll weevils are estimated to have caused $20 billion in damage.

Farmers used pesticides to fight boll weevils, but these chemicals alone were not enough to completely eliminate the pests. In the 1960s, scientists discovered that insects produce chemical substances called pheromones. Male boll weevils can sense pheromones made by female boll weevils. They follow the pheromones in order to find mates.

Scientists recreated these pheromones in a lab. Then they used the lab-created pheromones to lure boll weevils into traps. With the male beetles trapped, females were unable to reproduce. The boll weevil population dropped quickly, especially when combined with newer and more powerful pesticides.

In 1995, the US government approved GMO cotton to be grown commercially. Scientists added genes to the crop so that it would be more resistant to pests and herbicides. By 2020, about 96 percent of US cotton was GMO.

HARVEST AND USES

Most cotton harvests take place from August to October. Before harvesting the bolls, farmers spray chemicals on the crops.

Machine pickers create bales as they harvest.

Ginning machines can rapidly process large amounts of cotton.

The chemicals cause the leaves to fall off the plants, leaving only the bolls intact. This makes the harvest easier.

Once the leaves have fallen, farmers use one of two types of machines to harvest cotton. Most US cotton is harvested using machine pickers. These machines collect cotton only from open bolls. Machine strippers are the other type of machine used to harvest cotton. These machines strip all of the bolls from the cotton plant, regardless of whether the bolls are open or closed. The closed bolls become a waste product.

After machines harvest the cotton, the material is ginned. During this process, cotton seeds are removed from the fiber. The fibers are cleaned and shaped into bales. Cotton fibers are assessed for strength and color. They are primarily used to make textiles and clothing.

The crop's seeds are useful too. They can be made into cattle feed. Cotton seeds can also be processed to create oil that is used in many products, including soaps and cosmetics.

Flax produces flowers with five petals that may be blue, white, or pink.

FLAX

Flax is an herb-like plant. It grows to be about 3 to 4 feet (0.9 to 1.2 m) tall. Pollinated flax flowers develop bolls with seeds. Fibers from the bolls and stems are used to make textiles. Flax was first planted for its fiber more than 5,000 years ago, making it one of the oldest fiber crops in the world.

Flax should be planted in areas that receive full sun. It does best in fertile soils but can survive in slightly sandy soils. Flax should not be planted in heavy, clay-like soil. For a high-quality crop, flax should be watered regularly but not drenched.

FLAX IN THE UNITED STATES

Flax was an important fiber crop in the early days of the United States. However, production began declining in the

1940s as cotton became a more significant fiber crop. Globally, flax is primarily used for its fiber. Today in the United States, flax is mostly grown and harvested for its seeds, which are eaten and used in industrial products. In 2021, flax was grown on 268,000 acres (108,460 ha) of US land, with North Dakota and Montana being the top producers.

Flaxseed is high in dietary fiber, which can make it good for digestive health.

Flax matures 100 to 110 days after planting.

HARVEST AND USES

Flax is ready to harvest in August, when the bolls begin to crack open. For the fibers, the timing of the harvest is important. The longer farmers wait to harvest, the thicker the flax fibers will be. If flax is harvested too early, the fibers will be extremely fine and the seeds will be too immature for planting. If flax is harvested too late, the fibers will be too brittle to be used in textiles.

Farmers use combines to harvest flax. The machines cut the bolls from the rest

of the plant. The bolls are left to dry. After the bolls are dry, the flaxseeds can be removed. Retting is the next step. The flax is soaked in water during the retting process. This loosens the fibers so they can be separated and spun into thread. This thread is woven into linen cloth.

By harvesting time, the flax plant is dry and brown.

HEMP

Hemp is an herb. It has small, greenish-yellow flowers that produce seeds. These plants can grow to be 16 feet (4.9 m) tall. They are grown primarily as a fiber crop. The fibers for textiles are found in the stalks of the plant.

Hemp grows best in mild, humid climates. The crop should be planted in loamy soils. Hemp needs 25 to 30 inches (64 to 76 cm) of water each year. These plants require between 10 and 12 hours of sunlight a day. Hemp grows easily, often outcompeting surrounding plants. Because of this, weeds are generally not an issue when growing hemp.

Hemp's height helps it outcompete weeds.

Hemp's connection to marijuana, *pictured above*, has long made it a controversial crop.

GROWING HEMP IN THE UNITED STATES

It was once illegal to grow hemp in the United States. This is because hemp is related to the marijuana plant. Both plants produce a chemical called tetrahydrocannabinol (THC). THC causes people to feel high. However, hemp has significantly less THC than marijuana.

In 2018, the US government passed legislation called the Farm Bill. Among other changes, the bill removed many restrictions on hemp production. In 2020, reports on US hemp production were limited, but researchers estimated that $4.6 billion of hemp products were made. Approximately 33.2 million pounds (15 million kg) of US hemp were used for fiber in 2021.

HARVEST AND USES

The timing of the hemp harvest varies depending on what the crop is used for. When the crop is harvested for its fiber, it is harvested after about 70 days. Seed harvests occur several weeks later, after the seeds have fully matured.

An acre (0.4 ha) of hemp can produce 1,300 pounds (590 kg) of fiber.

Hemp ropes are known for being strong and durable.

To make textiles from hemp, the plants are cut at the stalks. The stalks are then put through a process called retting to break the fibers away from the rest of the stem. They are either left in the field and kept damp by dew, or they are placed in vats to soak in water. Moisture is needed for the retting process. After a few weeks of retting, the stalks are dried and crushed so that only the long fibers remain.

Hemp fibers are longer and stiffer than flax fibers. Hemp is also a darker color than cotton or flax and is not easily dyed. It is mainly used for products such as twine, rope, and canvas fabrics.

OIL CROPS

Canola is grown in many places, including the United States, Canada, Australia, Europe, and China.

CANOLA

Canola is a plant that grows to about 5 feet (1.5 m) tall. The plant has yellow flowers that produce pods with small seeds. Canola is related to mustard plants, broccoli, and cauliflower. Canola seeds are rich in oil, making canola plants a valuable oil crop.

Canola is a modified version of rapeseed. Canadian researchers bred rapeseed plants in the 1960s. They wanted to get rid of erucic acid in rapeseed oil. This acid can be toxic in high amounts. The researchers were successful in their breeding and named the new plant *canola*. The word is a mixture of the words *Canadian* and *oil*. In the United States, canola oil must contain less than 2 percent erucic acid. In 2013, GMO canola accounted for 95 percent of the crop in the United States.

Canola plants grow best in soils with high amounts of sulfur. For this reason, agriculture researchers recommend adding sulfur to soil before planting. The plants need about 20 inches (51 cm) of water as they grow. They need at least six hours of sunlight each day.

Canola plants need plenty of direct sunlight to grow well.

CANOLA IN THE UNITED STATES

Farmers may rotate their crops. They grow different crops in a field from season to season. Some farmers add canola to the rotation. Canola can improve soil health. Many farmers have reported larger harvests for crops planted in fields that were previously used for canola. The benefits are seen in the growing season immediately following the canola harvest.

Two types of canola are grown in the United States. Spring canola is planted around March and harvested in September.

Winter canola survives cold temperatures and thrives in the following growing season.

Canola seed pods contain about 20 to 30 tiny, round seeds.

Winter canola is planted in the fall and harvested the following summer. Most of the canola grown in the United States is spring canola. However, winter canola tends to produce a greater yield than spring canola.

Approximately 2 million acres (809,000 ha) of canola are grown in the United States each year. In 2021, canola was planted commercially in 29 states. North Dakota was the top producer.

HARVEST AND USES

Canola is ready to harvest when the seed pods become dry and rattle when shaken. The seeds will be dark brown or black, but the stalks of the plant remain slightly green. Combines cut canola plants and separate the seeds from their pods.

The seeds are then taken to processing facilities where waste such as stems and pods are removed. At the facility, canola seeds are heated and cooked. These steps increase the amount of oil that can be extracted from the seeds. Finally, the seeds are crushed, and oil squeezes out. The leftover seed material can be used to feed livestock.

Canola oil can be used for cooking. Scientists consider canola oil to be a healthy oil because it has a low percentage

Farmers must monitor their canola crop to determine the best time to harvest.

Canola oil is the second-most popular cooking oil in the United States.

of saturated fat, which is an unhealthy type of fat. Canola oil can be processed further to create biofuels. To create biofuels, natural plant oils undergo a chemical process. This process changes the chemical makeup of the natural plant oils. Canola-based biofuels can be mixed with diesel fuel to power vehicles and other equipment.

South Dakota is a major state for ethanol production.

CORN

Field corn can be used to produce an alcohol called ethanol. In 2021, the United States was the world's leading producer of ethanol. It produced more than 15 billion gallons (56.8 billion L) of ethanol that year.

ETHANOL USES AND PRODUCTION

Ethanol has many uses. It can be added to gasoline to make the fuel less polluting. More than 98 percent of US gasoline is mixed with ethanol. The substance is used in other products too. Ethanol is found in alcoholic beverages. It is added to cleaning products. It is also found in beauty products, including hair spray.

Ethanol is made through a process called fermentation. This is when yeasts and other tiny organisms are used to break down sugars. The sugars in corn are transformed into ethanol as they are broken down. This process is done in industrial plants. Many ethanol plants are located in the Midwest.

A type of fuel called E-85, made of a high percentage of ethanol, is often listed separately on gas station signs.

PEANUTS

Peanuts have a high oil content. Approximately 50 percent of a peanut's weight comes from oil. Because of this, peanuts are an important crop in the biofuel industry. One acre (0.4 ha) of peanuts can produce more than 100 gallons (380 L) of biofuel. However, peanuts require more water than other crops that can be made into biofuel.

Like other oil crops, peanut oil must be transformed before it can be used in vehicles. Chemicals are added to peanut oil. These chemicals separate usable fuel from other compounds in the peanut oil.

When used for cooking, peanut oil is good for frying food.

LOOKING AHEAD

In 2022, the oil company Chevron announced that it was partnering with agricultural researchers in Texas to develop peanut varieties that could produce even larger amounts of biofuel. Researchers hoped to produce peanuts that had an oil content of 60 percent. An acre (0.4 ha) of these peanuts could make 350 gallons (1,325 L) of biofuel.

Peanuts are also called groundnuts. The plants flower above ground, while their stems and seeds grow underground.

SOYBEANS

The United States is one of the top producers of soybeans. Soybeans are the major crop used to make oil. A chemical process transforms soybean oil into a biofuel. About 90 percent of agriculture-based oil produced in the United States comes from soybeans.

In cooking, soybean oil is used for frying, baking, and roasting.

The amount of soybean acreage in the United States grew 18 percent between 2002 and 2022.

ENVIRONMENTAL CONCERNS

Biofuels release less greenhouse gases than petroleum-based fuels, such as gasoline. For this reason, the United States is seeking to increase the use of biofuels. However, biofuels are expensive to produce. Some environmentalists have also calculated that increasing biofuel production with current technology may not have environmental benefits. For example, increasing soybean production may result in deforestation to clear lands for crops.

There are nearly 70 species of sunflowers.

SUNFLOWER SEEDS

Sunflowers are a type of herb. They have thick, hairy stems. The plants have yellow flowers that face toward the sun as they grow. As the flowers mature, they produce seeds.

Many varieties of sunflowers are grown. The largest can grow up to 15 feet (4.6 m) tall. The flowers can be up to 12 inches (30 cm) across. The oilseed sunflower is the type most commonly grown for oil production. It has a higher oil content than other sunflower varieties.

Sunflowers require full sun. They grow best in sandy, loamy soils. These plants can tolerate some drought-like conditions. However, they should be watered regularly in the weeks before and after they flower. They need about 1 inch (2.5 cm) of water each week during the growing season.

SUNFLOWERS IN THE UNITED STATES

In 2020, more than 2.98 billion pounds (1.4 billion kg) of sunflowers were grown in the United States. That year, North Dakota and South Dakota were responsible for approximately 84 percent of US sunflower production. The majority of sunflowers grown in the United States are harvested for oil.

Each sunflower head has up to 2,000 seeds.

HARVEST

Sunflowers are ready to harvest when the backs of the flower heads change from green to a yellowish brown. The heads should also droop slightly forward. The seeds should be black with white stripes.

Farmers use combines to harvest sunflower seeds. Combines separate the seeds from the rest of the plant. These seeds are further processed to produce oil. They are cleaned and the shells are removed. The inner parts of the seeds are ground up and heated. A machine presses on the seeds, squeezing out the oils. Chemicals may be added to the seeds to extract even more oil. These chemicals are boiled out at the end of the process, leaving only sunflower oil. This oil is often used for cooking.

Trailers carry sunflower seeds away from the fields for processing.

Sunflower oil is also one of the many types of plant-based oils that can be transformed into biofuels. Like other plant-based oils, a chemical process transforms the sunflower oil into biofuel. This biofuel can then be blended with diesel.

OTHER USES FOR SUNFLOWERS

Sunflower seeds have other uses besides oil and biofuels. After oil is extracted, the remaining material can be used as animal feed. Some types of sunflower seeds are sold as bird feed.

About 10 percent of sunflower seeds are grown for people to eat. The highest-quality seeds are roasted in their shells and may be salted or flavored. Sunflower seeds can also be made into sunflower butter and other products.

Sunflower oil is a popular choice for roasting or sautéing foods.

Sunflowers themselves are sold as decorations. They are popular garden plants. People may plant sunflowers to attract pollinators. Farmers may plant sunflowers to lure pests away from vegetables or other crops.

ORNAMENTAL CROPS

Ornamental crops may be grown or displayed in individual pots.

Ornamental crops are grown and sold for their beauty. In 2021, US ornamental crops brought in more than \$6 billion. These crops include cut flowers, garden plants, and houseplants. Commercial growing of ornamental crops is often done in greenhouses.

Ornamental crops can be organized into several categories based on their leaves, the length of their growing seasons, and whether the plants are grown for indoor or outdoor use. Some of the primary categories for US ornamental plants are annual garden plants, herbaceous perennial plants, and plants for indoor use. Many types of plants are within each category.

ANNUAL GARDEN PLANTS

Annual plants are those that last for only a single growing season. They usually die in the winter, when temperatures become too cold. Gardeners must replace them each year. Begonias and pansies are among the major ornamental crops in this category.

BEGONIAS

Begonias are popular garden plants that are relatively easy to grow. These flowers bloom in the summer and can last for several weeks. About 2,000 types of begonias are grown. They can be a variety of colors, including pink, red, and white. Different varieties have blooms of different shapes and grow in a range of sizes.

These plants grow in well-drained, slightly acidic soil. Experts recommend using peat-based soils to grow begonias. The plants should be grown in partial or indirect sun. Too much sunlight causes begonias to lose their flowers earlier. People should water their begonias once a week, once the top 0.5 inches (1.3 cm) of soil becomes dry. Overwatering begonias can cause their roots to weaken and rot.

In 2020, the US begonia industry was valued at more than $36.9 million. Michigan was the top grower of begonias. More than 180 growers accounted for more than 20 percent of US begonia sales.

Begonias are resistant to deer and rabbits, making them less likely to get eaten up in gardens.

PANSIES

Pansies can be grown in pots or garden beds. They are an option for gardeners who are looking for a late-blooming plant. When planted in the fall, pansies can flower before the first frost. Because these plants are somewhat resistant to cold weather, they can also be planted in the early spring. People who plant pansies in the spring may see their plants produce a second round of blooms in the fall. They can trim off dead flowers to encourage this growth.

Pansies have heart-shaped flowers with overlapping petals. Their petals are brightly colored, and some varieties have two-colored petals. For example, a petal may have a dark

Even a small planter of pansies can add a pop of color to a balcony or window.

Commercial growing of pansies may be done in greenhouses.

purple center and pale pink outer edges. Pansies come in many other colors, including yellow, white, and blue. Pansies do not typically grow larger than 8 inches (20 cm) tall and 6 inches (15 cm) wide.

People should plant pansies in full or partial sun. Pansy blooms last longer if planted in slightly shaded areas. Pansies do not like to be overcrowded. The plants should be spaced 6 to 12 inches (15 to 30 cm) apart. Pansies prefer loose soil with plenty of nutrients. People can add fertilizer to encourage growth. Soil should be kept moist. If pansies are planted in pots, people should make sure the water is able to drain to keep pansies healthy.

Pansies are a major annual garden plant grown in the United States. In 2020, pansies brought in approximately $52.2 million. Texas was the top-producing state.

HERBACEOUS PERENNIAL PLANTS

Herbaceous plants are those without woody tissues. They include many perennial plants, which are able to survive through multiple growing seasons. The aboveground portions of herbaceous perennial plants die during the winter. But the roots continue growing. When temperatures warm, new growth appears aboveground.

CHRYSANTHEMUMS

Chrysanthemums, or mums, are popular for their autumn blooms. They bloom as the days get shorter. Chrysanthemum flowers have many petals in a number of colors, including purple, orange, and red. Different varieties of chrysanthemums also have flowers of different sizes. At full size, these plants are about 3 feet (0.9 m) tall and 3 feet (0.9 m) wide.

Mums are best planted in the spring. This gives them an entire growing season to establish deep roots that can last through the winter. Chrysanthemums should

Chrysanthemums originated in China.

Chrysanthemum seedlings require attentive care to survive.

be spaced 18 to 36 inches (46 to 91 cm) apart. People should plant them in well-ventilated areas. They should water them at their bases and avoid getting the leaves wet. Regular watering is important to keep chrysanthemums healthy. The plants will stop growing if they do not get enough water.

Chrysanthemums need a lot of nutrients to survive. For this reason, experts suggest adding fertilizer to the soil every month. People who want their flowers to grow as big as possible should pinch off smaller buds. This helps make sure the large buds get as many nutrients as possible.

In 2020, nearly 50 million chrysanthemum plants were sold in the United States. In total, the plants were worth approximately $158 million. North Carolina was the top-earning state.

HOSTAS

Hostas are grown primarily for their foliage. They come in many varieties, making them a good choice for most gardens. Though many have teardrop-shaped leaves, other varieties may have differently shaped leaves. They come in many shades of green. In addition, different types of hostas have various growth rates and reach a range of sizes when fully grown. The largest hostas may grow to be 4 feet (1.2 m) tall.

The climate in almost every region of the continental United States is suitable for growing hostas.

When gardeners plant multiple hostas, they should plant them with enough space in between for the mature plants to not crowd each other.

People find that hostas are relatively easy to grow. These plants grow in full or partial shade. Hostas do not need to be watered often. Soil should be kept moist, but not wet. Hostas can tolerate short periods of drought. Growers report that hostas grow best when watered infrequently with a large amount of water. People can add fertilizer to soil to help hostas grow quickly.

In 2020, more than $36 million worth of hostas were sold in the United States. There were more than 750 commercial producers of hostas that year. New Jersey, Michigan, Ohio, and North Carolina were the top states for hosta production.

Ferns are put in hanging pots as decorations.

FERNS

Ferns are another perennial plant grown for their attractive foliage. They have lace-like leaves called fronds. More than 12,000 types of ferns are grown worldwide. Unlike other plants, they do not need pollination to reproduce. Instead, they release spores that fall to the ground and grow.

People can plant ferns at any time in temperate climates. In colder areas, it is best to plant them in early spring or summer. Ferns require little care throughout the year. People can trim away dead or unhealthy fronds early in the growing season to encourage new growth.

Because there are many types of ferns, most people are able to find a plant that suits their needs. Some ferns thrive in the shade. Others need full sun to survive. People should also check how large their fern will grow. Small ferns may grow to only 1 foot (0.3 m) tall. Large garden ferns may reach heights of 6 feet (1.8 m).

Slugs are a problem for gardeners who are trying to grow ferns. These pests feed on fronds. People can place slug bait that will kill slugs if eaten. They can also spray slugs with a salty spray. This will cause the slugs to slowly lose moisture and die.

Ferns are commercially grown in many states. Texas and California were the main growers in 2020. That year, the two states combined to sell about one-third of US ferns.

Ferns can provide shade and reduce erosion in addition to being beautiful additions to a landscape.

PLANTS FOR INDOOR USE

Not all plants are sold to be grown outdoors. Some sellers produce plants that are meant to be kept indoors. Research shows that adding greenery to an indoor space can boost creativity and reduce stress. Some indoor plants, such as orchids and poinsettias, are selected for their flowers. Others liven up a room with their lush foliage.

FLOWERING PLANTS

Orchids and poinsettias are two of the most popular flowering indoor plants grown in the United States. Both plants are grown in pots. In 2020, these two plant types combined for more than $433 million in sales.

Wild orchids are mostly found in tropical regions, but they are kept indoors around the globe.

Earth has more species of orchids than species of birds and mammals combined.

Scientists have identified more than 28,000 types of orchids. Some of these orchids can be grown at home. In general, orchids have irregularly shaped flowers with three petals. One of the petals is known as the lip. It has a different shape than the other petals and may have a pitcher-like shape. Orchids also have three petal-like structures called sepals that enclose the true petals. These plants have broad leaves.

Orchids come in a wide range of colors. Some of the most popular varieties are pink, purple, and white. Orchids can be challenging to grow because they need a lot of sunlight to encourage blooms. However, direct afternoon sunlight can damage blooms. Orchids grow best in humid conditions. They should be placed in areas with good airflow. People should keep orchids at temperatures between 50 and 85 degrees Fahrenheit (10 and 29°C).

Red poinsettias are popular winter holiday plants because of their color. Though brightly colored, the red parts of the plant are not flowers. They are leaves. In addition to red, these leaves can be a variety of colors, including white, pink, and orange.

People should place poinsettias in indoor areas that receive plenty of sunlight. These plants do best in temperatures between 65 and 70 degrees Fahrenheit (18 and 21°C) and are sensitive to temperature changes. Poinsettia pots should allow water to drain, as sitting water can cause damage to roots. The plants should be watered when the surface of the soil is dry to the touch.

Poinsettias originated in Mexico and Central America.

A terrarium can hold multiple succulents, creating a decorative display.

FOLIAGE

In 2020, more than $756 million worth of indoor foliage plants were sold in the United States. Many varieties are grown. They grow to different sizes and require different levels of care. Beginners and advanced growers can find a plant that suits their space and skill level.

A 2020 survey found that aloe vera was the most popular indoor plant in the United States. This plant has thick green or gray leaves. It produces a gel that is used in medicines. Aloe vera is a type of succulent. Succulents grow naturally in warm deserts around the world. Like other succulents, aloe vera should be kept in warm temperatures and need plenty of sunlight. They do not need to be watered often. One reason aloe vera and other succulents are popular is because they are easy to care for.

Snake plants are another popular, low-maintenance foliage plant. These plants are named for their sword-like leaves that look similar to snakes. Many types of snake plants have striped leaves or a yellow outer border. Snake plants grow slowly. They can grow in sun or partial shade. These plants do not need much water and should be watered only when the soil is dry to the touch. During winter, they can survive without water for two months.

Snake plants should be kept where children and pets cannot reach them because these plants are toxic when eaten.

More advanced growers may add a fiddle leaf fig to their homes. These small trees have large leaves with wavy edges. These plants are known for being sensitive. They should be placed by a window that receives plenty of filtered sunlight throughout the day. People can wipe down the leaves of the plant to clean off dust. This helps the fig receive as much sunlight as possible. These trees grow best in warm, humid environments.

Growers should water fiddle leaf figs when the top inch (2.5 cm) of soil becomes dry. They should make sure pots are well-draining, as sitting in water will damage the plants. Fiddle leaf figs are sensitive to both underwatering and overwatering. Growers can check the plant's leaves to see if it is receiving the correct amount of water. If the leaves turn brown along the edges and fall off, the tree is not getting enough water. Overwatered fig trees will have leaves with dark brown spots and brown edges.

The fiddle leaf fig is a type of ficus plant.

GLOSSARY

acidic
Having the qualities of an acid, an often sour-tasting substance that reacts with other chemicals.

climate change
Long-term shifts in temperatures and weather patterns.

commercial
Relating to farming with the goal of producing goods for sale or profit.

dormant
Temporarily inactive.

export
A good produced in one country and sold in another.

foliage
The leaves of a plant.

hybrid
The product of mating between animals or plants of different species or types.

loamy
Made up of a mixture of clay, silt, and sand.

machete
A large knife.

organism
A living thing.

pollinate
To carry pollen from one plant to another.

protein
A nutrient found in many plants and animals that is necessary for survival.

semiaquatic
Partially on water and partially on land.

temperate
Having temperatures that are neither too hot nor too cold.

textile
Fiber or cloth.

variety
A specific group of plants.

vulnerable
Capable of being easily damaged.

yield
The amount of a crop that is grown in a given season.

TO LEARN MORE

FURTHER READINGS

Debbink, Andrea. *Flowers and Plants*. Abdo, 2022.

McKinney, Donna B. *The Tractor and Equipment Encyclopedia*. Abdo, 2025.

O'Brien, Cynthia. *The Impact of Food and Farming*. Crabtree, 2020.

ONLINE RESOURCES

Booklinks
NONFICTION NETWORK
FREE! ONLINE NONFICTION RESOURCES

To learn more about farming and crops, please visit **abdobooklinks.com** or scan this QR code. These links are routinely monitored and updated to provide the most current information available.

INDEX

PHOTO CREDITS

Cover Photos: Shutterstock Images, front (apple blossom, grapes, peanuts, pumpkins, hay bale, sunflower, wheat); Jeff Smith/Shutterstock Images, front (corn stalks); Vas Kondr/Shutterstock Images, front (strawberries); Olesia Bech/Shutterstock Images, front (tomatoes); Andrei Dubadzel/Shutterstock Images, back (alfalfa); Maks Narodenko/Shutterstock Images, back (corn)

Interior Photos: Jiang Hongyan/Shutterstock Images, 1, 155; Shutterstock Images, 2–3, 5, 7 (bottom), 10, 14, 16–17, 19, 20, 23, 24–25, 25, 27, 28, 36, 37, 38–39, 39, 40, 44–45, 46–47, 47, 52, 54–55, 55, 56–57 (bottom), 60, 62, 62–63, 64, 68, 69, 70, 71, 72, 73, 74, 78, 80–81, 82–83, 84, 85, 87, 88, 90, 94, 94–95, 96, 97, 98–99, 99 (left), 99 (right), 100, 102–103 (top), 104–105 (top), 110–111, 111, 112–113, 114, 115, 118–119, 121, 123, 125, 126, 128, 129, 130–131, 131, 141, 148–149, 152–153, 153, 154–155, 156, 160, 164, 165, 166, 166–167, 169, 170, 171, 176, 177, 178, 179, 181, 184, 187; David McNew/Getty Images News/Getty Images, 6; Olly Plu/Shutterstock Images, 7 (top); Ksenia Ragozina/Shutterstock Images, 8–9; Sheila Fitzgerald/Shutterstock Images, 11, 93; Tommy Lee Walker/Shutterstock Images, 12–13; Oleksandr Katrusha/Shutterstock Images, 13; Volodymyr Maksymchuk/Shutterstock Images, 15; Dima Moroz/Shutterstock Images, 17; Maria Kazakova/Shutterstock Images, 18; Edgloris Marys/Shutterstock Images, 21; Jim West/Science Source, 22; Lena Platonova/Shutterstock Images, 26; M. Unal Ozmen/Shutterstock Images, 29; VL Studio/Shutterstock Images, 30–31 (top); Lijuan Guo/Shutterstock Images, 30–31 (bottom); Olivier Le Queinec/Shutterstock Images, 32; Glenn Price/Shutterstock Images, 32–33; Lukasz Szwaj/Shutterstock Images, 34–35 (top); Alexandra Latypova/Shutterstock Images, 34–35 (bottom); Tom Werner/DigitalVision/Getty Images, 40–41; Dieter Hawlan/Shutterstock Images, 42; David Moreno Hernandez/Shutterstock Images, 43; Drazen Zigic/Shutterstock Images, 44; Elena Masiutkina/Shutterstock Images, 48; Tony Savino/Corbis Historical/Getty Images, 49; Africa Studio/Shutterstock Images, 50–51; Olga Nikiforova/Shutterstock Images, 51; Sue Smith/Shutterstock Images, 53; Ricardo Ninin/Shutterstock Images, 56–57 (top); HUM Images/Universal Images Group/Getty Images, 58–59; Wellford Tiller/Shutterstock Images, 59; Hurst Photo/Shutterstock Images, 61; Maksim Safaniuk/Shutterstock Images, 65; Trong Nguyen/Shutterstock Images, 66; Zulkarnieiev Denis/Shutterstock Images, 67; Paulo Nabas/Shutterstock Images, 75; Tony Campbell/Shutterstock Images, 76–77; Igor Dutina/Shutterstock Images, 77; Peter Zijlstra/Shutterstock Images, 79; Paul Maguire/Shutterstock Images, 81; Billion Photos/Shutterstock Images, 83; Bear Productions/Shutterstock Images, 86; Anny Ta/Shutterstock Images, 89; Mark Elias/Bloomberg/Getty Images, 90–91; Luke Sharrett/Bloomberg/Getty Images, 92; Lynne Ann Mitchell/Shutterstock Images, 101; Richard Panasevich/Shutterstock Images, 102–103 (bottom); White Field Photo/Shutterstock Images, 104–105 (bottom); Repina Valeriya/Shutterstock Images, 106–107; V. S. Anandhakrishna/Shutterstock Images, 107; Orest Lyzhechka/Shutterstock Images, 108–109; Andrei Dubadzel/Shutterstock Images, 109, 133; Andrii Horulko/Shutterstock Images, 113; George Clerk/E+/Getty Images, 116; Deyana Stefanova Robova/Shutterstock Images, 117; Red Herring/Shutterstock Images, 119; Marko Kukic/Shutterstock Images, 120; Nancy Bauer/Shutterstock Images, 122; Ruslan Suseynov/Shutterstock Images, 124–125; Jurgis Mankauskas/Shutterstock Images, 127; Tomasz Klejdysz/Shutterstock Images, 132; Erika Norris/Shutterstock Images, 134; Atlas Studio/Shutterstock Images, 135; Kedson Carvalho/Shutterstock Images, 136; Yerbolat Shadrakhov/Shutterstock Images, 137; Edu Mungga/Shutterstock Images, 138; Cloud Cap Photography/Shutterstock Images, 139; Manee Meena/Shutterstock Images, 140; Phillip Minnis/Shutterstock Images, 142; CRS Photo/Shutterstock Images, 143; Caleb Holder/Shutterstock Images, 144; Carlos Rudinei A. Mattoso/Shutterstock Images, 145; Sundry Photography/Shutterstock Images, 146; Paul R. Jones/Shutterstock Images, 147; Mara Ze/Shutterstock Images, 149; Artic Photo/Shutterstock Images, 150–151 (top); Stephen Mcsweeny/Shutterstock Images, 150–151 (bottom); Darryl J. Smith/Shutterstock Images, 157; Cristi Savin/Shutterstock Images, 158–159; Stefan Sutka/Shutterstock Images, 159; Scott Olson/Getty Images News/Getty Images, 161; Jim Parkin/Shutterstock Images, 162–163; Daniel J. Macy/Shutterstock Images, 163; Irina Mos/Shutterstock Images, 168–169; Kirillov Alexey/Shutterstock Images, 172; Simona Pavan/Shutterstock Images, 173; Lapa Smile/Shutterstock Images, 174; Kimberly Boyles/Shutterstock Images, 175; Kitti Gavinratchatarot/Shutterstock Images, 180; Steve Bower/Shutterstock Images, 182; Nataliya Nazarova/Shutterstock Images, 183; Dzina Belskaya/Shutterstock Images, 185; Adam Yee/Shutterstock Images, 186

ABDOBOOKS.COM

Published by Abdo Reference, a division of ABDO, PO Box 398166, Minneapolis, Minnesota 55439.

Printed in China.
052024
092024

THIS BOOK CONTAINS RECYCLED MATERIALS

Editor: Arnold Ringstad
Series Designer: Colleen McLaren
Production Designer: Joshua Olson

LIBRARY OF CONGRESS CONTROL NUMBER: 2023949528

PUBLISHER'S CATALOGING-IN-PUBLICATION DATA

Names: Lim, Angela, author.
Title: The crop encyclopedia / by Angela Lim
Description: Minneapolis, Minnesota: Abdo Reference, 2025 | Series: Farming encyclopedias | Includes online resources and index.
Identifiers: ISBN 9781098294311 (lib. bdg.) | ISBN 9798384913580 (ebook)
Subjects: LCSH: Crops--Juvenile literature. | Field crops--Juvenile literature. | Horticulture--Juvenile literature. | Soils and crops--Juvenile literature. | Agriculture--Juvenile literature. | Farming--Juvenile literature. | Encyclopedias and dictionaries--Juvenile literature.
Classification: DDC 633--dc23